BITE MARKS ON MY CEILING FAN

bite marks on my ceiling fan

KINSEY MCINTYRE

CONTENTS

~ *VII*

~19~

Whisper
53

To my parents, for teaching me that I don't need to be anyone but myself

~ 1 ~

SONGBIRD

S ongbird, the peach is bruised
    its skin is blemished
its color is gone

songbird, there's no use
the fruit has rotted
outside and in

why try, songbird?
your voice will crack when the skin breaks
and the juice pours out brown instead of bright

the innards will coat your throat
liquid forced down tight
just because it was once good, songbird, doesn't mean it never
changed

i ask you again, songbird
does it please you to feel pain?
to know that your brothers and sisters' songs will be sweeter
now that yours has gone bad?

sunrise, songbird
remember that which you love so?

the orange and pinks—
peach
you love it for the peach, don't you?

it reminds you of ripeness, songbird
of youth and fulfillment
so you look down at this peach—
this rotted, ruined peach—
and you see the sunrise that was this morning
now gone into oblivion
along with the song you have always despised having to sing

are you tired of sweetness, songbird?
being chirped at for your melancholy tunes
ones that are more truthful than your fair weather friends'?

i'm sorry, songbird
i will put my knife away
i will leave the bruises on the peach
and i will watch you eat

i will see the sunrise in your eyes

songbird, the peach is bruised
but i know now that so is your song

~ 2 ~

PAINT CHIPS

I used to write prayers across my polka dot walls. Now I peel the paint off with my teeth to know what its like to hold holiness underneath my tongue—a dissolving pill of past purity.

God liked to talk to me when I was younger, more naive. I think I actually knew more as a child than I do now. Love made more sense when my father held my hand than when he raised it against me.

He's never tried to hit me. Sometimes I wish he would.

It would be easier to feel the way I do about my dad if he left bruises. Broke bones instead of promises, gave me pain instead of hope. I occasionally nod off to the thought of myself in his embrace and trying to ignore the blood dripping down from the knife in the base of my spine. My vertebrae will heal about as quickly as my bleeding heart.

I keep in my eyes the sparkle of childhood—though now it moreso resembles the flash of a camera capturing a moment that I don't wish to see. I am the audience and the performer, the script and the orchestra. I write the words and speak the words but do I feel the words? Do I feel what I think or do I think what I've been told? I tend to think that the first thought crossing my mind is what I've heard, and the next what I know.

"I love him."

"I have to."

God is my best friend, but sometimes I wish He would leave bruises, too. Is God not the father of all fathers, after all?

Maybe if the Lord gave him a son instead of a me, I wouldn't ache for the sanctity of paint chips in my throat.

~ 3 ~

GOD AND COFFEE

Jamie sometimes thought that she just might believe in God.

This isn't a story about God, but it is a story about Jamie. And faith. And a lot of things that one might associate with God, but will hopefully start associating with this story: Jamie's story.

It was mid-March in a town that city people would call desolate and residents would call home. The trees were still recovering from their seasonal suicide, the flowers on their way to blooming once again.

Jamie thought that if God was real, he did a good job making flowers.

The weight of a mug dangled from her fingers, precariously balancing between her palm and pinky. The ceramic scalded her hands, but the nerve endings in her appendages had been scorched to a point of no return long ago. Coffee did that to a person.

Jamie was thinking about God, and faith, and all of the things related to God and faith as her fingers lost feeling, just as they did every morning since she was eleven. Coffee did that to a person.

A slam echoed through the house, and she barely felt the sting of steaming liquid sloshing against her skin as she flinched at the sound of clobbering footsteps coming down the stairs. It wasn't uncommon to see Jamie flinch; coffee did that to a person.

She didn't turn around as the racket made its way into the kitchen. She didn't turn around when she heard the coffee pot detach from its stand, and she didn't turn around when a chair scraped loudly against the linoleum floors. She only turned around when a throat cleared from behind her, and she took a sip of the drink that gave her an ounce of confidence for every ounce she sipped. Coffee did that to a person.

"I'm sorry about last night," her father said gruffly, lifting the cup to his mouth and slurping so loudly that Jamie had to hold back her cringe. "You know it's hard for me, with work and everything. It won't happen again."

Jamie pursed her lips, just for a millisecond, before she let a blinding smile cross her face. "I know, Dad. It's alright"

He nodded, eyes peering into his mug almost as if he thought if he stared hard enough, he could keep his promise. The father only needed caffeine when he had his moments. That's what Jamie called them: moments. Because when you have moments, it takes something small to convince yourself that it was just that. Not a condition. Not a common occurrence. A mistake. So when he stared down at a cup sitting on a table with chipped paint, Jamie watched and let herself believe that if she did the same, that if she stared hard enough into the mug that burned her hands and made her feel something other than the nothing that she had made begrudging friends with over the years, that he might be telling the truth this time.

Coffee did that to a person.

God wouldn't have made coffee if he was real.

~ 4 ~

BITE MARKS

My room is green. It used to remind me of the outside I could only see and never touch. It eventually lost its poetry.

There are bite marks on my ceiling. I don't remember making them. I can only touch the plaster between my gapped teeth and put the pieces together with what I was given.

I don't own a ladder.

Sometimes I think I die in my sleep and leave hints to alive-me about what the afterlife is like. I don't like calling it the afterlife. Isn't anything after just a continuation of what was? There's no after or before, just what is and what might be.

My molars are stuck somewhere in the insulation. My incisors are lodged in a lightbulb. But when I run my fingers across my lips all that comes off is whispered promises of belonging. My veins bleed red but they remain blue on my skin, the same way I come off strong and feel so very weak. My fingernails hurt every morning. I wake up with wood wedged into my cuticles. I don't know what I'm trying so hard to grab onto.

A room covered in scratches and teeth is one most wouldn't dare to venture into, but I sleep there every night. My room is green. It used to remind me of the outside I could only see and never touch.

It lost its poetry when the walls turned red.

It wasn't from the blood of my womb or my arteries, however both wept ruby tears at the sight. No, the blood came from heaven, from a God of many languages yet so few words. I don't know why the Lord chose my bedroom to die in. It seems an odd place for a God to leave His world behind. But God chose to be God, and maybe He regretted that. Maybe He regretted His lack of humanity and did the most human thing of all—lost.

The blood is falling down the walls.

I think God left the bite marks on my ceiling.

I don't own a ladder.

~ 5 ~

ALIEN

I am an alien stuck on a planet of people that know I'm an alien but won't admit it.

~ 6 ~

GIRLS/ORANGES

i met a girl once
   a stranger to me
a stranger to herself

she kept her nails short
polish clear
used them to peel oranges with deft movements and swift
 hands
she always shared them with me

i never ate the slices
(i don't like oranges—
never have)
but i fed them to the ducks at the pond where we sat

there was a bench we sat on each week
one with a plaque on the back
"we were friends and we were love—
was there ever truly a difference?"

the girl and i never talked
not once did a word leave our lips
but we shared oranges
and we sat on a bench made with love

and we allowed those weights on our shoulders—
the ones that didn't allow us to speak—
to turn into wings

we stopped coming to the bench one day

we became the birds we fed

we flew away

~ 7 ~

ABEL

my uncle raises cows. not to sell, but to have–to watch and to raise. i don't know why he doesn't sell them–i can only imagine he would make a fortune due to just how many calves he's brought up. my only assumption is that he likes the power.

one of his cows was pregnant–twins. she gave birth to a set of boys. i can only ever remember cain and abel, jacob and esau when i think of those boys. one loved and coddled by a mother, one left to fend off the world.

abel hasn't been eating.

i'm playing with my cousin outside when a calf raises up from the grass, knobbly knees barely peeking out from above the weeds. he is midnight black. i can't pick out his eyes from the darkness of his face. his tongue makes an appearance every now and again, the only way i can determine his mouth from his neck.

my cousin doesn't notice him; he's two years old. older than abel, younger than his mother, though not by much.

the calf stares at me. i stare back.

he didn't eat yesterday. my uncle said he was too busy staring at his brother–cain, with his strong legs and full belly. i wonder how cows recognize their family. is it by appearance? by feeling? by the sanctity of their bond? the blood of the covenant is thicker than the water of the womb, so i doubt divinity is the answer.

abel doesn't look away from my face. i don't know why he noticed me; i'm seventeen years old, older than his mother, much older than abel himself. i've never worked with animals before, nor do i know anything about abandonment.

i think the calf knows, though, that i understand being outdone by a brother.

i have a brother. two years younger, one head taller. we've been engaged in a silent, weaponless battle since the day he was born. fighting for attention.

abel is standing at the fence. it's electric. i always tell my cousin not to get too close or he'll be shocked. i let myself stand. the baby is playing in the grass, paying no attention to me or my movements.

i make my way over to his post. abel skitters back, legs too long for his small body tangling in a morbid sort of dance as he scrambles away. i hold out a hand. hesitantly, he leans forward, letting his nose meet my palm.

i take a step closer.

abel doesn't move.

nudging my hand with his snout, abel pushes my fingers until they're pointing somewhere to the right. i turn.

cain is with his mother, feeding.

abel steps closer to me.

i feel a new instinct inside of me flare to life. the one that tells me to reach through the fence and pull abel close to my chest. ignore the electricity from the wire swarming through my veins and let him sink deep, deep, deep into my bloodstream where he will always be warm. let him swim through the valleys of my heart so he will always have a home to come back to, one that pulses with love and laughing arteries. i ache for pressure in my chest; a pressure that negates clogged vessels and rigid bone. i ache to give him the love of a mother, the kind he never had. the kind he aches for.

i tell him that in whispers. i think for a moment that he understands me, his head tilting up, eyes wide and knowing. dark, dark gaze piercing that empty space i now hold, a space i did not know was empty until moments ago.

cain passes by behind abel, but the calf doesn't turn. he keeps his eyes on me. cain sounds his call. abel stares ahead.

i can only watch as abel steps forward.

once.

twice.

cain sounds again.

abel nudges my hand off of his head.

presses his neck to the electric fence, body shaking with the force of the shocks. does it again and again and again until his small, wise body falls to the grass in a sad mimicry of a seizure.

his body can't take it.

i don't know if i can take it.

my hand has a few fine black hairs littered across it when i look down. the baby is crying. i think i'm crying, too. is that wailing coming from me? is that my mouth open, dripping with sorrow and the first death of a mother, a mother who was never supposed to die twice?

his mouth is foaming now. his body is still. his leg thumps the ground with the aftershocks every now and again.

the baby is crying.

cain is crying.

his mother doesn't move.

i wrap my hand around the fence.

~ 8 ~

...

I don't remember the last time I read what I wrote.

~ 9 ~

SICK

I keep in my heart the knowledge that I am capable of all things until I convince myself otherwise. It is not a simple thing to know, but it is an easy thing to feel.

I am sick. I know I am sick. But I have so wholly convinced myself that it is a sickness unable to be healed that I can no longer separate myself from the illness that haunts me. I am flanked by shadow and trailed by light, the two refusing to mix yet remaining suspiciously close, almost as if neither wants to lose me to the other. I lean towards the warmth of the sun and linger in the darkness of the moon. One is to keep me safe, one is to keep me hidden. You would think I knew which one was which by now.

I live in a world free of magic. Not by conquest or elimination, solely by lack. I can see the wondrous in the eyes of those around me, but I have never found a wand that sparked fire or a hat that birthed a rabbit.

My sickness makes me believe in magic.

Sometimes I don't. Sometimes I can distinguish the ocean from a river. Other times, though, I only see the fish swimming upstream and not the width of the water. All this to say, I was born with narrow sight and the most open of minds.

Does this make sense?

I've been told I write the way I speak—in parables and makeshift riddles. I have a poet's mouth, they say. I have also been told that the words that leave my mouth and the tips of my fingers linger in the minds of others, refusing to grant them peace. I only wish to grant peace to those who find it in my words. Those who seek it there will find it; those who do not will only find nonsense.

I write this to spell out what few things I know. Magic is sometimes real, my words are loud, and my demeanor is quiet. My illness is always real, but it can feel worse or better than it is. There is no happy medium in sickness.

It is not a simple thing to know, but it is easy to feel.

~ 10 ~

ISAAC

i climbed a tree once
    when i was small
  and still fit snugly in the branches

  i would pick bark from the trunk
  scratch prayers into the skin with the trees own limbs
  peeling layer after layer off
  talking to God with sticks and rocks

  i found peace in nature's cradle
  listening to the lullaby of a mother bird
  the song of the wind
  i felt infinite when up in the sky

  nobody could reach me in the sky

  it made me think about Jesus-
  how He lived an earthly life before finding his place in the
heavens
  was He lonely now?
  was the sky—though belonging to him—anything more than a
barrier between Him and His children?

  but maybe the earth was His prison

a place He was made to live and die on
a world that would never love Him as much as He loved it
Jesus was a carpenter
His father the creator
ironic. isn't it?

God created the earth His son would die on
does it really matter that He created the son as well?

abraham asks isaac when he climbs in a tree
"do you think God will let you come down?"

isaac answers—
"do you think i will wait for an answer before i do?"

~ 11 ~

MONSTER IN THE MIRROR

there is a monster in the mirror, and all she wants is to go home.

she once told me that the mirror is where she has always lived, so i'm not quite sure where "home" is. she keeps a hand pressed to the glass and her eyes aimed at me at all times. i don't know where she casts her stare when i'm not in the room, and i always have wondered what lingers in her mind. what do monsters imagine when left to their own devices? do they dream of destruction or redemption?

some part of me knows that it is both. a little voice in the back of my mind tells me that she wants to demolish every part of herself, to rebuild her body and spirit into something completely unlike her beginning. or maybe she regrets the middle more than anything. maybe the start is where she thrived.

i don't remember when i started calling her a monster. she didn't used to be one. she was youthful and gorgeous and smiled every time she saw me. now, fangs peek from behind her pale lips and her broad brows furrow when i come into view.

i wonder now if she had always been a monster. maybe she was just better at hiding it then.

my fingers fiddle with the curtain draped over the only mirror in my room. it is tall and narrow, just wide enough for the monster to stand with her arms at her sides. the corner of the curtain is frayed from where my hands pick and pull at it. with bated breath, i yank it off of the mirror.

the monster is crouched on the ground, one hand braced on the wooden edge of the glass. her teeth are bared and her face is scrunched, looking at me with malice in her muddy eyes.

i can't help but make the same face in return.

~ 12 ~

ASHES

a sh floats down slow
    coating the driveway and my mother's outstretched hands
she looks as if she's praying
like she's waiting for God to touch her palms and erase
the flames
let them soak into her skin instead of the walls of our home

mama, i wonder sometimes if i died in that fire
i was only a baby at the time
but i remember enough to know—
know that you would be better off if that blaze
 had sucked me in

i know you would always mourn your baby girl
the one who died in the midst of the only home she
had ever known besides the womb
but you would only have to grieve what
could have been
not what was
not what is

you wouldn't have to cry over the daughter that
couldn't live—just the one who didn't survive

i am the daughter you never wanted, mama
no matter how much you deny it
i will never be that little girl again
the one who watched ashes fall like butterfly wings
fluttering and lifeless
wonder in her eyes and fear in her heart

i will forever be the daughter who died at fourteen
instead of the baby that could have been your world

does this make sense, mama?
does it worry you that i still write like this, despite being bet-
ter?
i might be mostly healed, but i will always be scared
scared of what will happen when you realize i will
always need you more than you need me

mama, do you wish i had burned?
cremated before i could walk?
i know your answer would be no
never in a million eternities would you agree with a
word on this page
but mama—
my darling mama—
don't you think i would be better off as a memory?

~ 13 ~

GOD + THUNDER

There is plaster from my ceiling in between my teeth. I don't remember leaving the bite marks on the interior of my roof, but I can tell it was me due to the sizable gap between the two front teeth.

I sleepwalk a lot. I don't remember it when I wake up. I don't own a ladder that reaches my ceiling.

I try not to sleep a lot. The doctors tell me it's insomnia—I tell them God speaks in my dreams more than He did in the Old Testament.

Avoiding sleep isn't hard when your mattress is on the floor. I prefer my chair. I can't sleep sitting up, my breathing becoming more erratic and choked. When I somehow manage to fall asleep in the chair, my own snoring tends to wake me up. It is loud and unsettling for most—including myself.

God snores, too.

He calls it thunder, the sounds He makes while sleeping. There is always thunder somewhere in the world. He likes to tell me that rain is nightmares and sunshine is dreams. Sometimes I wonder why God has so many bad dreams. Can't He just rid himself of the memories that plague Him, or does the plague infect Him as well?

~ 14 ~

NOT MY NAME

y our first breath was a warning
        a smoke signal in a hospital room
an omen of ravens and crows

i held you close to my chest
dread in my heart and love on my face
your fingers barely curled around one of mine
and i thought—
is this how a mother feels?

powerless and in need?
ruined and burdened?
i never thought i would feel my baby as a stone
over my heart instead of a human being
but here—
in this room—
i am alone

my mom smiles down at me
with something in her eyes
"congratulations, mama"

i want to bark back
want to scream

because mama's not my name

~ 15 ~

FEELING SMALL

i am sitting in the library with my baby cousin.

he is playing with scarves and singing songs with a woman who shares my name–not my real one, but the one i chose. he does his best to sing along but his vocabulary and his voice are not quite vast enough at his mere two years of age. his arms and legs flail in a strange little dance that makes the others laugh.

it doesn't make me laugh.

i'm too busy doing my best to make myself smaller in the children's chair i'm sitting in. it's already a mockery of the size i used to be, who i used to be. my arms fold against my chest and my legs cross over one another. i slouch.. i keep my eyes on my cousin, but my mind is on the girth of my feet in my shoes, the width of my palms and the square of my knees. my shoes used to be smaller than this. my palms used to have fewer lines. my knees used to be knobbly and too big for my legs, but now they're just too big. they are covered in a layer of fat that didn't used to be there before.

my cousin is giggling. he is small. tall for his age, but small. i wish i was small.

the woman tells the children to go color on the paper she has laid out for them. my cousin bounds over, sitting in my aunt's lap and using a broad grip to hold his crayon. his hands are chubby and cute. i look down at my own.

my fingers are too large. long and fat, nails barely taking up any space. i flex them. my knuckles make a crackling sound. i wince.

my cousin looks up at me. his eyes are still too big for his face–everyone says he's going to grow into them soon. he reaches out for me.

i look down at my hands.

~ 16 ~

MAMA

i am sitting on the kitchen counter. mama stands on the fluorescent-illuminated tile next to me, peeling an orange. her hands work at the fruit deftly. she offers me half without looking up, the habit of providing sinking deeper into her bones with each movement of her fingers.

i take it, popping the citrus into my mouth and humming at the taste. mama smiles at the sound, but her eyes are blank. not empty, but blank. i know what that look is. i've seen it all my life.

a bead of juice pours from the corner of my lips. she wipes it away with her thumb.

blank.

my mama excels at that. remaining perfectly imperfect. she can quietly dissuade the attention from her own person onto her children, the way every parent does but not every parent wants to.

i wonder sometimes if my mama wants that attention.

mama peels the other half of the orange. i've always found that strange; the way that she peels one half and gives it away instead of undoing the whole skin at once.

"why do you do that?" i keep my voice soft, not wanting to break the careful quiet we've stuffed in between the crevices of the cabinets and underneath the placemats.

she looks up at me. "do what?" she asks, voice just as low, but i know she understood the first time i asked.

"why do you always peel one half before the other?"

mama smiles up at me, lips crooked. "because i'm a mother."

but did you want to be?

i'm staring at a wall made of glass, peering through at rows of babies in plastic bassinets. a hospital, my mind provides helpfully. the pediatric ward. my eyes scan across the names pasted to the front of each one, until i finally land on a name i recognize.

a man appears next to me, a solemn look on his face but pride in his eyes. we're looking at the same baby.

"which one is yours?" he asks, voice gruff and somehow wistful. i point at a random child, one with a blue hat and pouted lips. my eyes never leave the girl with the butterfly on her blanket.

the man nods. my grandfather points at my mother and says, "that one's mine."

i nod. "she has your eyes." it's a lie. she doesn't right now, but she will. the man puffs out his chest anyways.

"she looks just like her mother to me," he tells me. i can't help but look away, over at the man that would break the woman who broke me. i can see my mother in his eyes, not the ones i look into every day but the ones i see in pictures. pictures from a time long gone.

his eyes are not yet blank, but they will be.

a crinkling hits my ears. i look down. my grandfather has a plastic bag in his hand, and i can make out something round inside. he follows my gaze. smiles.

"my wife loves oranges," he tells me, reaching into the bag. he pulls out a fruit and reaches out his arm. "want one?"

i take it. i peel one half before the other.

no one will hurt my mama.

i'm in the backseat of dad's car. mama sits in the front seat, facing the window. her arms are crossed over her chest. my headphones sit snugly over my ears. no music is playing.

"you aren't listening," dad starts. "do you hear what i'm saying? does this even bother you?"

mama doesn't move, but i see her eyes flicker down. i can't tell what she's looking at.

my dad slams a hand down on the steering wheel. she doesn't jump. she's used to this.

i don't jump either.

i can see my dad peer at me through the rearview mirror. i don't look up. i know if i did i would only see myself reflected back at me. the anger in our eyes was different, but it was anger nonetheless.

mama looks out the window again. her eyes are different from mine. i don't know how else to say it.

i got my dad's half of the orange.

i'm staring at mama's eyes again when she looks down once more. she looks at her left hand.

i turn on my music.

my grandfather takes me to meet his wife. i still have orange juice on my fingers, but i do my best to wipe it off on my jeans. i'm older here. my hair is shorter. i can see myself still, looking through the glass at my dad's eyes and mama's mouth. rageful and silent.

my grandmother is still in a hospital gown. sweat lines her brow but her lips are smiling. she eyes the denim residue sticking to my hands with something close to disdain. her husband raises the bag in his hand. she connects the dots.

handing her an orange, the man sits down by her bedside. i blink. i remember seeing this, when she was dying. but now an empty bassinet is at her side instead of the woman who raised me.

"who might you be?" she asks. her fingers look like mama's as she peels the fruit.

i give my name. it's odd. i can see myself in them but they don't see me at all.

my grandfather explains how we met. i say that the baby with the blue hat and the pout is my estranged sister's, that this is the first time we have seen each other in a while, and it is also most likely the last. they frown. i shrug. it doesn't hurt. i've never had a sister.

a nurse knocks on the door, a bundle in her arms. my heart clenches when i see how the woman and man light up, because i know it won't last long before that light goes dark.

mama is cleaning the floors for the third time today.

she hasn't complained once. not when dad trekked in with muddy shoes and never stopped to apologize. not when the dog rolled across the kitchen tile and left clumps of hair in her wake. not when i dropped my cup of orange juice and fell to my knees to clean it up. she only placed a hand on my shoulder to pull me to my feet and asked me to empty the mop bucket outside.

i'm sitting at the kitchen table now, a fresh cup of juice in my hands. i tap the glass with my fingernail.

tap, tap, tap

i look.

mama's arms are lined with tension. they tremble with every sweep of the mop.

tap, tap, tap

her eyes are still, unmoving in their sockets, not even glancing at the wet socks on her feet after water sloshes out of the bucket.

tap, tap, tap

tap tap tap

taptaptaptaptaptaptaptap

the mop snaps in half.
mama's eyes don't look down.

mama liked me. i had never been good with kids, but mama liked me.

her parents had apparently deemed me suitable to be around their daughter. we had dinner every saturday night, mama peering around at us with the purest of joy in the eyes she got from her father. i felt her happiness in those moments. those small blips of time where she got to see the three of us together, the ones who would raise her and the one she would raise.

it was the first time her father had drank since her birth.

grandma didn't like it when he drank, but she never told me that. she just looked at me with that strained smile of hers and gave a little shake of her head. "don't mention it," the smile said. "it's not worth it."

i couldn't find it within myself to say anything; it wasn't my business, despite it being my family. that's the problem with secrets-they can only haunt the one who keeps them.

eventutally, however, the bruises on the woman's face and the tear tracks on mama's cheeks became too hard to ignore.

i came over unannounced on a sunday morning. they used to call it "God's day" when they talked about it, but i had noticed grandma brushing the topic aside when i asked them about church. i couldn't ask their church friends if they had been going-that's the problem with dreams. you can only haunt the ones who caused them.

i didn't knock. the door was unlocked-they lived in a good neighborhood, no one locked their doors, they always said.

the best neighborhoods always had the bloodiest of carpets.

mama was on the ground. that was the first thing i noticed.
i always noticed her first.

the second thing i noticed was that grandma was beside her, cradling her head in her hands and letting the quietest sorrow i had ever heard pour from her silent lips.

i know now where mama got them from.

the man was passed out in the chair across from them.

the first thing i did was pick up mama. grandma was too weak. she was young, but weakness doesn't always come from age.

the second thing i did was pull grandma to her feet. she wobbled before collapsing once again. she didn't say a word when her knees met the carpet. silent lips never wailed.

the third thing i did was place a kiss on grandpa's cheek.

i always noticed mama first.

i walked out with judas on my mind, the smell of stale beer in my nose, and a baby in my arms.

i don't like loud noises. i got that from mama.

the birthday party is loud. my dad is drinking again. there's a bottle on his lips and laughter on his tongue.

he's not a happy drunk, though.

i hold onto mama's arm, fielding off touchy family members with forced smiles and too-tight hugs. she does the same. i learned from her, after all.

mama tugs on my hand. she leads me to the couch in the corner, letting me sit down before she settles down beside me. dad looks over. he's laughing. his eyes aren't.

mama looks down at her left hand.

"i wouldn't be mad," i whisper. she doesn't hear me. asks me to speak up.

"your ring is pretty," i say instead, not having enough courage to repeat myself. because i got my mouth from her, and my eyes from dad.

i know they're sad-my eyes, that is. i know i look like a kicked puppy. mama knows it, too. she just strokes my arm. says, "i know," in the voice i used the first time.

i can hear her.

grandma gives me custody of mama. she doesn't say anything when she signs the papers. just adjusts the bulky sunglasses on her face and walks away.

she doesn't sign the other set of papers i sent her.

mama adjusts to life with me easily. she likes my house. says it makes her feel like a princess because its so big. "like a palace," she tells me.

she grows up under my care. her hair gets longer, the way grandma never let her keep it. the way mama never let me keep mine. she goes to school. she makes friends.

she comes home crying.

i ask her what's wrong.

"they told me i would make a good mother," she babbles through tears. i flinch. she doesn't notice. "they-they said that i would be an amazing wife."

i know what's wrong. she's twelve. she still remembers.

"you don't have to be either of those things, you know," i whisper. my heart breaks in my chest. i can see the hope in her eyes. her own heart swells. "you don't have to be what they want."

she tells me she doesn't want a husband. she screams until her throat is hoarse that she's never having children, that she's never going to ruin someone by making them have a mother like her.

mama is twelve.

i feel younger than i am.

my hair is growing longer

i don't know how old i am.

mama divorces dad the first time he hits me.

she gives me the ring.

she knows i hate the thing. but she gives me the ring.

the girl grows up. i don't remember anything other than her name. i used to call her something else. i don't know why. she has a name.

she turns sixteen. she tells me when she has her first kiss, says she hated it. she's sure she doesn't want to get married. i don't know why it hurts when she says that.

i tell her things change. she tells me some things are meant to stay the same.

i help her decorate her cap for graduation. she paints it with oranges and blooming flowers. it tickles something in my mind, but i can't put my finger on it. she tells me they remind her of me. i cry. she laughs. says i've always been too soft when it came to her.

i walk her across the stage at her school. she cries. i laugh. say she's always been too soft when it came to things like this.

we go home and eat ice cream on the kitchen floor. i wake up the next morning to the smell of citrus. i don't remember ever waking up before, i realize. how strange.

she's sitting on the kitchen counter eating an orange. she peels the whole thing at once, a continuous strip of rind falling to her palms.

she doesn't offer me half.

i wipe the juice from her lips.

a girl with long hair and a ring around her neck looks down at me.

"mama?"

~ 17 ~

IT'S QUIET OUT HERE

i t's quiet out here.

i am sitting under a concrete canopy that separates the two parts of my house. my dog is licking the edges of her water bowl; the other one is barking up a tree. the third sits inside my grandmother's room, rolling in the comfort of a plush bed and air conditioning. i just watch.

my fingers tap away on my keyboard. nearly silent underneath the chirping of the bird nearby. nearly.

my mind feels akin to the bird at this moment. repetitive. loud. telling me things i know not to be true, but sound a lot like fact after enough crowing. because maybe, it tells me, just maybe–

i listen to the squirrel skittering across the roof.

no one needs to listen to my mind. most of all me.

it knows all of my nooks and crannies. it knows where the vein across the top of my foot ends and the lines on my hands begin. it can tell the difference between my left eye and my right, because i'm the only one who knows one is crooked.

my mind could tell you the day my parents stopped loving and started worrying—yes there is an overlap but there is also a difference.

it's quiet out here.

it's never quiet when my family is home—the tv is always blaring and my mom is always chattering on the phone. my brother's basketball is always thump, thump, thumping across the slab out in the yard. i miss the sound now.

i think my dogs can tell when i'm sad.

the youngest barks less—only does it when anyone comes near me. the oldest stares.

i think the oldest got that from me. i've never known what to do when someone i love is upset—always just holding their hand and waiting for an adult to come along to do the soothing. to be fair, i'm not usually the reason someone is crying. i'm just the one that made it worse.

i can feel the breeze starting to chill my skin. it's the beginning of october and only the wind is cold, not the air. i let my hands stop for a moment. feel. let the cold penetrate my bloodstream and sink into my bones. it's easy being cold.

mama used to tell me that for a summer baby i sure have always hated the heat. i always responded that being conceived in november must have done a number on me.

it's quiet out here.

i went to the store with my dad today, before they left. he made fun of me for the music i picked in the car.

there's no music out here.

i could play some—my phone is right there—but that would ruin the sounds. the birds and the dogs and the trees and the grass. i wish there was rain.

i've never liked the rain, but the rain makes good quiet.

~ 18 ~

DISGUISE

there has always been a feeling, one i have not been able to name. the one that sits heavy in my chest, like a log in a quiet wood or a rock in the river. as i look along the pattern of this feeling throughout my life i realize it has only ever been grief in different disguises. i am grieving the people i will never let go of, the guilt that will haunt me for decades. i am grieving what never was but what could have been, and, most of all, i am grieving me. i am grieving the version of myself i imagined in my childhood, the one with a mind capable of magic and a heart so kind and tender. i have grown up to be jaded and i lack all whimsy, but that little girl is always there as a whisper in my mind and i will grieve her as well. i will forever be held in the palm of someone who does not know me, the one who knows me least of all, because she does not allow herself to be seen. i will forever be held in my own hand.

~ 19 ~

WHISPER

i can't decide if i'm too much of a person or not enough.

not my humanity, no, i know how human i am. i empathize and love and hate and do all of the things that humans do. but i have forever been unable to understand how i touch the world. do i touch it with my hands? my voice, my words, my feet on the ground? or am i the voice and not the one who releases it, simply a sound that brushes the tops of the trees and fades into the wind? maybe i am the wind. maybe i am the one who shakes branches and steals voices and turns over houses. a breeze would probably be more accurate, wouldn't it? i have never had the lack of human-ity necessary to knock over trees and flood the streets.

but i think i could whisper.

Kinsey McIntyre is a young author with a passion for the written word. She hopes to become an author who can display her name proudly for the work she has done.

Milton Keynes UK
Ingram Content Group UK Ltd.
UKHW030656181124
2908UKWH00038B/367

9 798330 543861